C000022364

DON'T PANIC

YOU'RE ONLY

60!

summersdale

DON'T PANIC, YOU'RE ONLY 60!

An Hachette UK Company
www.hachette.co.uk

Summersdale Publishers Ltd
Part of Octopus Publishing Group Limited
Carmelite House
50 Victoria Embankment
LONDON
EC4Y 0DZ

www.summersdale.com

Printed and bound in the Czech Republic

ISBN: 978-1-78685-295-3

Substantial discounts on bulk quantities of Summersdale books are available to corporations, professional associations and other organisations. For details contact general enquiries: telephone: +44 (0) 1243 771107 or email: enquiries@summersdale.com.

TO.....................

FROM...................

CONTENTS

ANOTHER YEAR

OLDER

—

I'M 60 YEARS OF AGE.
THAT'S 16 CELSIUS!

—

GEORGE CARLIN

I WAS ALWAYS TAUGHT TO
RESPECT MY ELDERS AND
I'VE NOW REACHED THE
AGE WHEN I DON'T
**HAVE ANYBODY
TO RESPECT.**

George Burns

FOR ALL THE ADVANCES IN MEDICINE, THERE IS STILL NO CURE FOR THE COMMON BIRTHDAY.

JOHN GLENN

A DIPLOMAT
IS A MAN
WHO ALWAYS
REMEMBERS
A WOMAN'S
BIRTHDAY

BUT NEVER REMEMBERS HER AGE.

Robert Frost

THE BEST BIRTHDAYS OF ALL ARE THOSE THAT HAVEN'T ARRIVED YET.

Robert Orben

ON THE LAST DAY OF MY 59TH YEAR I WAS TREMBLING WITH ANTICIPATION. I'VE HEARD SO MUCH ABOUT THE SWINGING SIXTIES – I COULDN'T WAIT TO GET STUCK IN!

Anonymous

OUR BIRTHDAYS
ARE FEATHERS
IN THE BROAD
WING OF TIME.

JEAN PAUL RICHTER

YOU'RE NOT 60.
YOU'RE 18 WITH 42
YEARS' EXPERIENCE.

Anonymous

FROM OUR BIRTHDAY, UNTIL WE DIE,

IS BUT THE WINKING OF AN EYE.

W. B. Yeats

WHATEVER WITH THE PAST HAS GONE, THE BEST IS ALWAYS YET TO COME.

Lucy Larcom

—

IF WE COULD BE TWICE
YOUNG AND TWICE OLD
WE COULD CORRECT
ALL OUR MISTAKES.

—

EURIPIDES

EVERY YEAR ON YOUR
BIRTHDAY, YOU GET
A CHANCE TO
START NEW.

Sammy Hagar

I HAVE
EVERYTHING I
HAD 20 YEARS
AGO, ONLY IT'S
ALL A LITTLE
BIT LOWER.

Gypsy Rose Lee

YOU CAN'T
TURN BACK
THE CLOCK,

BUT YOU CAN
WIND IT UP
AGAIN.

Bonnie Prudden

JUST WHAT I
ALWAYS
WANTED

YOUTH IS THE GIFT OF
NATURE, BUT AGE IS
A WORK OF ART.

Garson Kanin

YOU KNOW YOU
ARE GETTING OLD
**WHEN THE
CANDLES**
COST MORE THAN
THE CAKE.

BOB HOPE

WE KNOW WE'RE
GETTING OLD WHEN
THE ONLY THING
WE WANT FOR OUR
BIRTHDAY IS NOT TO
BE REMINDED OF IT.

Anonymous

**YESTERDAY
IS HISTORY,
TOMORROW
IS A MYSTERY,
BUT TODAY
IS A GIFT.**

THAT IS WHY IT IS CALLED THE PRESENT.

Eleanor Roosevelt

THERE ARE 364 DAYS
WHEN YOU MIGHT GET
UN-BIRTHDAY PRESENTS...
AND ONLY ONE FOR
BIRTHDAY PRESENTS,
YOU KNOW.

LEWIS CARROLL

ALL THE WORLD IS
A BIRTHDAY CAKE, SO
TAKE A PIECE, BUT
NOT TOO MUCH.

George Harrison

A TRUE FRIEND
REMEMBERS YOUR
BIRTHDAY BUT
NOT YOUR AGE.

Anonymous

—

A FRIEND NEVER
DEFENDS A HUSBAND
WHO GETS HIS WIFE AN
ELECTRIC SKILLET FOR
HER BIRTHDAY.

—

ERMA BOMBECK

BIRTHDAYS ARE GOOD
FOR YOU. STATISTICS
SHOW THAT THE PEOPLE
WHO HAVE THE MOST
LIVE THE LONGEST.

Larry Lorenzoni

SIXTY
IS THE
NEW 40!

Bill Maher

**GETTING OLD IS
A BIT LIKE GETTING
DRUNK; EVERYONE ELSE
LOOKS BRILLIANT.**

Billy Connolly

MEN ARE
LIKE WINE.
SOME TURN
TO VINEGAR,

BUT THE BEST

IMPROVE

WITH AGE.

C. E. M. Joad

I STILL HAVE A FULL
DECK; I JUST SHUFFLE
SLOWER NOW.

ANONYMOUS

AGE IS A
MATTER OF
FEELING, NOT
OF YEARS.

George William Curtis

**AT MY AGE I DO
WHAT MARK TWAIN
DID. I GET MY DAILY
PAPER, LOOK AT THE
OBITUARIES PAGE AND
IF I'M NOT THERE I
CARRY ON AS USUAL.**

PATRICK MOORE

MY IDEA
OF HELL
IS TO BE
YOUNG
AGAIN.

MARGE PIERCY

I SO ENJOY WAKING UP AND NOT HAVING TO GO TO WORK.

SO I DO IT THREE OR FOUR TIMES A DAY.

Gene Perret

**AGE IS AN ISSUE
OF MIND OVER MATTER.
IF YOU DON'T MIND,
IT DOESN'T MATTER.**

Anonymous

OLD AGE IS AN EXCELLENT
TIME FOR OUTRAGE.
MY GOAL IS TO SAY
OR DO AT LEAST ONE
**OUTRAGEOUS THING
EVERY WEEK.**

Maggie Kuhn

IT'S SAD
TO GROW OLD,
BUT NICE TO RIPEN.

Brigitte Bardot

ONE OF THE BEST PARTS OF GROWING OLDER? YOU CAN FLIRT ALL YOU LIKE SINCE YOU'VE BECOME HARMLESS.

Liz Smith

THERE IS ALWAYS A LOT
TO BE THANKFUL FOR, IF
YOU TAKE THE TIME TO
LOOK. FOR EXAMPLE, I'M
SITTING HERE THINKING
HOW NICE IT IS THAT
WRINKLES DON'T HURT.

ANONYMOUS

NO MATTER WHAT HAPPENS, I'M LOUD, NOISY, EARTHY AND READY FOR MUCH MORE LIVING.

Elizabeth Taylor

TIME AND TROUBLE
WILL TAME
AN ADVANCED
YOUNG WOMAN,

BUT AN ADVANCED
OLD WOMAN IS
UNCONTROLLABLE BY
ANY EARTHLY FORCE.

Dorothy L. Sayers

—

I'M NOT INTERESTED
IN AGE. PEOPLE WHO
TELL ME THEIR AGE ARE
SILLY. YOU'RE AS OLD
AS YOU FEEL.

—

ELIZABETH ARDEN

DO A LITTLE DANCE, MAKE A LITTLE LOVE

GROW OLD
ALONG WITH
ME! THE BEST
IS YET TO BE.

Robert Browning

THE MORE YOU PRAISE
AND CELEBRATE YOUR LIFE,
**THE MORE THERE IS IN
LIFE TO CELEBRATE.**

Oprah Winfrey

OLD PEOPLE AREN'T EXEMPT FROM HAVING FUN AND DANCING...

AND
PLAYING.

Liz Smith

I ALWAYS MAKE
A POINT OF STARTING
THE DAY AT 6 A.M. WITH
CHAMPAGNE. IT GOES
STRAIGHT TO THE HEART
AND CHEERS ONE UP.
WHITE WINE WON'T DO.
YOU NEED THE BUBBLES.

John Mortimer

A MAN OF 60
HAS SPENT
20 YEARS
IN BED
AND OVER THREE
YEARS IN EATING.

ARNOLD BENNETT

WITH MIRTH AND LAUGHTER LET OLD WRINKLES COME.

William Shakespeare

THERE COMES A TIME IN
EVERY WOMAN'S LIFE
WHEN THE ONLY THING
THAT HELPS IS A GLASS
OF CHAMPAGNE.

BETTE DAVIS

I'D HATE TO DIE
WITH A GOOD
LIVER, GOOD
KIDNEYS AND A
GOOD BRAIN.

WHEN I DIE I WANT EVERYTHING TO BE KNACKERED.

Hamish Imlach

THE OLDER I GET,
THE MORE I REALISE
THAT JUST KEEPING ON
KEEPING ON IS WHAT
LIFE'S ALL ABOUT.

Janis Ian

—

THERE IS NO PLEASURE
WORTH FOR GOING
JUST FOR AN EXTRA
THREE YEARS IN THE
GERIATRIC WARD.

—

JOHN MORTIMER

LET US CELEBRATE THE
OCCASION WITH WINE
AND SWEET WORDS.

Titus Maccius Plautus

IT'S
IMPORTANT
TO HAVE A
TWINKLE
IN YOUR
WRINKLE.

Anonymous

THE AGEING PROCESS HAS YOU FIRMLY IN ITS GRASP

IF YOU NEVER GET THE URGE TO THROW A SNOWBALL.

Doug Larson

AGE DOES NOT DIMINISH THE EXTREME DISAPPOINTMENT OF HAVING A SCOOP OF ICE CREAM FALL FROM THE CONE.

Jim Fiebig

ALTHOUGH
IT SOUNDS
ABSURD, IT IS
TRUE TO SAY I
FELT YOUNGER
AT 60 THAN I
FELT AT 20.

Ellen Glasgow

THEY SAY GENES
SKIP GENERATIONS.
MAYBE THAT'S WHY
GRANDPARENTS FIND
THEIR GRANDCHILDREN
SO LIKEABLE.

JOAN McINTOSH

MY GRANDMOTHER
STARTED WALKING
5 MILES A DAY WHEN
SHE WAS 60.

SHE'S 97 NOW,
AND WE DON'T
KNOW WHERE THE
HELL SHE IS.

Ellen DeGeneres

THERE IS NO
OLD AGE.
THERE IS,
AS THERE ALWAYS WAS,
JUST YOU.

CAROL MATTHAU

—

AGEING SEEMS TO BE
THE ONLY AVAILABLE
WAY TO LIVE A
LONG LIFE.

—

KITTY O'NEILL COLLINS

I DIDN'T GET OLD
ON PURPOSE, IT JUST
HAPPENED. IF YOU'RE
**LUCKY IT COULD
HAPPEN TO YOU.**

Andy Rooney

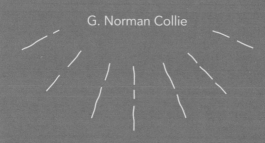

GRANDCHILDREN DON'T
MAKE A MAN FEEL OLD;
IT'S THE KNOWLEDGE
THAT HE'S MARRIED TO
A GRANDMOTHER.

G. Norman Collie

AN OLD-TIMER
IS ONE WHO
REMEMBERS
WHEN WE
COUNTED OUR
BLESSINGS

INSTEAD OF OUR CALORIES.

Anonymous

OLD AGE ISN'T
SO BAD WHEN YOU
CONSIDER THE
ALTERNATIVE.

Maurice Chevalier

I'M NOT YOUNG ENOUGH TO KNOW EVERYTHING.

Oscar Wilde

MEN DO NOT QUIT
PLAYING BECAUSE
THEY GROW OLD;
THEY GROW OLD
BECAUSE THEY
QUIT PLAYING.

OLIVER WENDELL HOLMES SR

IT TAKES A LONG TIME TO BECOME YOUNG.

Pablo Picasso

INSIDE EVERY OLDER PERSON IS A YOUNGER PERSON

- WONDERING
WHAT THE HELL
HAPPENED.

Cora Harvey Armstrong

WE ARE
ALWAYS THE
SAME AGE
INSIDE.

Gertrude Stein

—

OLD AGE IS
NO PLACE
FOR SISSIES.

—

BETTE DAVIS

OLDER AND WISER?

THEY TOLD ME IF I GOT
OLDER I'D GET WISER.
IN THAT CASE I MUST
BE A GENIUS.

George Burns

IF YOU ARE 60
YEARS OLD
AND HAVE
NO REGRETS,
YOU HAVEN'T
LIVED.

CHRISTY MOORE

THE OLDER I
GROW THE MORE I
DISTRUST THE FAMILIAR
DOCTRINE THAT AGE
BRINGS WISDOM.

H. L. Mencken

THE SECRET
TO STAYING
YOUNG IS TO
LIVE HONESTLY,
EAT SLOWLY,

AND LIE
ABOUT
YOUR AGE.

Lucille Ball

YOU ARE ONLY YOUNG ONCE, BUT YOU CAN BE IMMATURE FOR A LIFETIME.

John P. Grier

THE MIND THAT IS
WISE MOURNS LESS
FOR WHAT AGE TAKES
AWAY; THAN WHAT IT
LEAVES BEHIND.

WILLIAM WORDSWORTH

AGE IS A HIGH
PRICE TO PAY
FOR MATURITY.

Tom Stoppard

—

BECOMING A
GRANDMOTHER IS
WONDERFUL. ONE
MOMENT YOU'RE JUST
A MOTHER. THE NEXT
YOU ARE ALL-WISE
AND PREHISTORIC.

—

PAM BROWN

I DON'T WANT
TO RETIRE.

I'M NOT THAT GOOD AT CROSSWORD PUZZLES.

Norman Mailer

ONE OF THE GOOD
THINGS ABOUT GETTING
OLDER IS THAT YOU FIND
YOU'RE MORE INTERESTING
**THAN MOST OF THE
PEOPLE YOU MEET.**

Lee Marvin

EXPERIENCE IS THE NAME EVERYONE GIVES TO THEIR MISTAKES.

Oscar Wilde

THE FIRST HUNDRED YEARS ARE THE HARDEST.

Wilson Mizner

**IF I HAD MY LIFE
TO LIVE OVER AGAIN,
I WOULD MAKE THE
SAME MISTAKES,
ONLY SOONER.**

Tallulah Bankhead

**WHEN I WAS A BOY
THE DEAD SEA WAS
ONLY SICK.**

GEORGE BURNS

LIVE, LOVE

AND LAST

YOU ONLY LIVE ONCE, BUT IF YOU DO IT RIGHT, ONCE IS ENOUGH.

MAE WEST

—

SEIZE THE MOMENT.
REMEMBER ALL THOSE
WOMEN ON THE *TITANIC*
WHO WAVED OFF THE
DESSERT CART.

—

ERMA BOMBECK

PEOPLE ARE ALWAYS ASKING ABOUT THE GOOD OLD DAYS.

I SAY,
WHY DON'T
YOU SAY
THE GOOD
NOW DAYS?

Robert M. Young

LIFE CAN ONLY
BE UNDERSTOOD
BACKWARDS; BUT
IT MUST BE LIVED
FORWARDS.

Søren Kierkegaard

AND IN THE END IT'S
NOT THE YEARS IN YOUR
LIFE THAT COUNT.
**IT'S THE LIFE IN
YOUR YEARS.**

Abraham Lincoln

THERE WAS NO
RESPECT FOR YOUTH
WHEN I WAS YOUNG,
AND NOW THAT I AM
OLD, THERE IS NO
RESPECT FOR AGE –
I MISSED IT COMING
AND GOING.

J. B. Priestley

**MAY YOU LIVE
ALL THE DAYS OF
YOUR LIFE.**

Jonathan Swift

THE KEY TO SUCCESSFUL AGEING

IS TO PAY AS LITTLE
ATTENTION TO IT
AS POSSIBLE.

Judith Regan

TIME
DOTH
FLIT;
OH SH*T!

Dorothy Parker

THE PROBLEM WITH
GETTING OLDER IS YOU
STILL REMEMBER HOW
THINGS USED TO BE.

PAUL NEWMAN

—

THE OLD BEGIN TO COMPLAIN OF THE CONDUCT OF THE YOUNG WHEN THEY THEMSELVES ARE NO LONGER ABLE TO SET A BAD EXAMPLE.

—

FRANÇOIS DE LA ROCHEFOUCAULD

WHEN YOU ARE
DISSATISFIED AND
WOULD LIKE TO
GO BACK TO YOUR
YOUTH, THINK
OF ALGEBRA.

Will Rogers

ILLS, PILLS AND TWINGES

AS YOU GET OLDER THREE
THINGS HAPPEN. THE FIRST
IS YOUR MEMORY GOES,
**AND I CAN'T REMEMBER
THE OTHER TWO...**

Norman Wisdom

I DON'T FEEL OLD.
I DON'T FEEL ANYTHING
TILL NOON.
THAT'S WHEN
IT'S TIME
FOR MY NAP.

BOB HOPE

MY DOCTOR TOLD
ME TO DO SOMETHING
THAT PUTS ME OUT OF
BREATH, SO I'VE TAKEN
UP SMOKING AGAIN.

Jo Brand

ADVANCED
OLD AGE
IS WHEN
YOU SIT IN
A ROCKING
CHAIR

AND CAN'T GET IT GOING.

Eliakim Katz

AFTER YOU'RE OLDER,
TWO THINGS ARE
POSSIBLY MORE
IMPORTANT THAN ANY
OTHERS: HEALTH
AND MONEY.

HELEN GURLEY BROWN

I DON'T DO
ALCOHOL ANY
MORE – I GET THE
SAME EFFECT JUST
STANDING UP FAST.

Anonymous

I'M AT AN AGE
WHEN MY BACK
GOES OUT MORE
THAN I DO.

Phyllis Diller

—

I'M PUSHING 60.
THAT'S ENOUGH
EXERCISE FOR ME.

—

MARK TWAIN

PASSING THE
VODKA BOTTLE
**AND PLAYING
THE GUITAR.**

Keith Richards on how he keeps fit

NEVER WORRY ABOUT YOUR HEART TILL IT STOPS BEATING.

E. B. White

DON'T LET AGEING GET YOU DOWN.

IT'S TOO
HARD TO GET
BACK UP.

John Wagner

A HEALTHY OLD FELLOW,
WHO IS NOT A FOOL,
IS THE HAPPIEST
CREATURE LIVING.

RICHARD STEELE

IF YOU REST, YOU RUST.

Helen Hayes

EVERYTHING SLOWS
DOWN WITH AGE, EXCEPT
THE TIME IT TAKES CAKE
AND ICE CREAM TO
REACH YOUR HIPS.

John Wagner

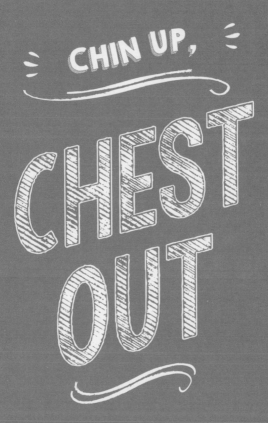

CHIN UP,
CHEST
OUT

I'M NOT SIXTY, I'M 'SEXTY'!

Dolly Parton

I DON'T PLAN TO GROW
OLD GRACEFULLY;
I PLAN TO HAVE
FACELIFTS UNTIL
MY EARS MEET.

RITA RUDNER

I HAVE A
FURNITURE
PROBLEM.

MY CHEST HAS FALLEN INTO MY DRAWERS.

Billy Casper

I'VE ONLY GOT ONE
WRINKLE AND I'M
SITTING ON IT.

Jeanne Calment

LET US RESPECT GREY HAIRS, ESPECIALLY OUR OWN.

J. P. Sears

**LOOKING 50
IS GREAT – IF
YOU'RE 60.**

Joan Rivers

SOME PEOPLE, NO MATTER HOW OLD THEY GET, NEVER LOSE THEIR BEAUTY – THEY MERELY MOVE IT FROM THEIR FACES INTO THEIR HEARTS.

Martin Buxbaum

THERE IS MORE
FELICITY ON
THE FAR SIDE
OF BALDNESS

THAN YOUNG
MEN CAN
POSSIBLY
IMAGINE.

Logan Pearsall Smith

YOU CAN
ONLY
PERCEIVE
REAL
BEAUTY IN
A PERSON
AS THEY
GET OLDER.

Anouk Aimée

HOW FOOLISH TO THINK
THAT ONE CAN EVER
SLAM THE DOOR IN THE
FACE OF AGE. MUCH
WISER TO BE POLITE AND
GRACIOUS AND ASK HIM
TO LUNCH IN ADVANCE.

NOËL COWARD

TO WIN
BACK MY
YOUTH...
THERE IS
NOTHING I
WOULDN'T DO

– EXCEPT TAKE
EXERCISE, GET
UP EARLY, OR
BE A USEFUL
MEMBER OF THE
COMMUNITY.

Oscar Wilde

YEARS MAY
WRINKLE THE
SKIN, BUT TO GIVE
UP ENTHUSIASM
WRINKLES
THE SOUL.

Samuel Ullman

—

AN ARCHAEOLOGIST
IS THE BEST HUSBAND
ANY WOMAN CAN HAVE:
THE OLDER SHE GETS,
THE MORE INTERESTED
HE IS IN HER.

—

AGATHA CHRISTIE

DON'T RETOUCH
MY WRINKLES IN
THE PHOTOGRAPH.
I WOULD NOT WANT
IT TO BE THOUGHT
THAT I HAD LIVED
FOR ALL THESE
YEARS WITHOUT
**SOMETHING TO
SHOW FOR IT.**

Queen Elizabeth, The Queen Mother

EXPERIENCE
IS A COMB
THAT LIFE
GIVES YOU AFTER
YOU LOSE
YOUR HAIR.

JUDITH STERN